Caleb Crosses the Country

A Camel's Tale

Written by Dan Taylor & Damon J. Taylor

Illustrated by Damon J. Taylor

Where Kids are number One

Caleb the Camel was scared of traveling. For you and me this might not be a big deal, but for Caleb it was a very big deal.

You see, God made camels able to travel very far across the wide, hot desert. He gave them long legs, big feet, and room for lots of water in a hump on their backs.

Caleb had everything he needed to take long trips like all the other camels, but he was afraid to leave home. And that's a big problem for an animal who was made to cross deserts.

HOME·SWEET HOME

Caleb liked his stall and he liked his family, but he didn't like change. He wanted things to always be the same. Changes scared him.

Traveling was full of changes. That's why Caleb was afraid to travel.

"I'm too frightened of everything out there to be of any use to anyone," Caleb thought sadly to himself.

"I don't see how God can use a camel like me. I can barely leave my stall to go to the market. How can I ever make a long trip like camels are supposed to?"

Caleb was still feeling sad when some Wise Men came to his stable.

These Wise Men had studied and learned many things. They knew from their studies of the stars that an important child was to be born in Bethlehem.

They also knew that a special star would lead them to the child. The journey would be long. They would need some camels. . . .

"We need some very good camels for our trip," the Wise Men told Omar.

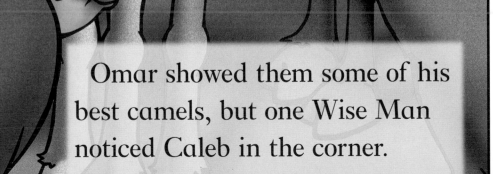

Omar showed them some of his best camels, but one Wise Man noticed Caleb in the corner.

"I'll take that one!" he declared. This was not what Caleb wanted to hear— the Wise Man was pointing right at him!

"Oh, no!" thought Caleb. "These men want me to go on their long trip to a new country. That sounds scary! I would have to leave my nice, safe stall and go into the desert. I'm too afraid to do that!"

And to show that he didn't plan on going *anywhere*, Caleb plopped right down in the straw.

"You look frightened, friend," the short little Wise Man said in a soothing voice. "I can understand that. Traveling can seem very scary, because it means leaving your nice, safe home.

"But we are not going on this trip alone. We are following a very special star. God put that star high in the sky and made it extra bright, just for us. He is guiding us with that star. He wants us to make this trip!"

"God wants these men to make a trip, and He wants me to go with them and help," Caleb thought. "That must mean that God can use me, even if I'm scared!"

This made Caleb feel much better. He stood up and smiled at the Wise Man. He was ready for the trip!

One day,
a terrible
sandstorm
blew in.

Robbers
attacked the
caravan.

A poisonous
snake invaded
the campsite.

CRAZY
OMAR'S NEW
AND USED CAMELS

The Wise Men stopped at
Crazy Omar's to get new
camels for their trip.

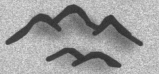

Some pretty scary things happened on their trip across the desert. But whenever he was scared, Caleb would look up at the star and remember the Wise Man's words: "God is guiding us with that star. He wants us to make this trip!"

Even though Caleb was very scared, he knew that God would take care of them.

The trip across the desert was very long, but for Caleb it seemed to go quickly. Each night the Wise Men followed the bright star . . .

. . . until at last they arrived in Bethlehem.

There they found a very special baby named Jesus, lying in a manger. The Wise Men bowed before the baby and worshiped Him. They gave to baby Jesus the precious gifts they had brought with them.

When Caleb saw how happy the Wise Men were, he didn't feel scared at all. He just felt very glad that God had been able to use him, Caleb, a camel who had been so afraid.

The End.

For Parents

Spiders. Darkness. Heights. Clowns. Everyone is afraid of something. The fears that begin in childhood often linger with us for the rest of our lives. It is important for our chilren to learn, early on, how to handle fear and keep it from ruling their lives.

A trip across the desert was a big change for Caleb and contained all kinds of scary "unknowns." But when he heard that God wanted him to be a part of this journey, he decided to give it a try. He knew that he needed to obey God, even if he was afraid. With the special star reminding him that God was watching over him, he didn't have to be afraid when scary things happened during the journey. In fact, he found out he actually *enjoyed* traveling.

Caleb's story reminds us all that obeying isn't always easy. Following God can involve risk. But no matter how hard or scary things seem, if we are doing what God wants us to do, then we can trust Him to take care of us. God was there for Caleb, and He'll be there for us, too.

Below are some questions to help you have a dialogue with your children about how the lessons Caleb learned can relate to them and their lives. After you finish talking, take some time to pray with your children. Ask God to protect them and to help them trust Him with their fears.

Discussion Questions:
- Do you like to travel? Tell about a trip you took. Did anything scary happen during the trip? Did you remember to trust God, even when you were scared?
- When scary things happened on Caleb's trip, the special star reminded him that God was taking care of him. Do you have a "special star," something that can help you remember that God is taking care of you?
- Have you ever been scared to do something, but you did it anyway? What happened?
- If God wanted you to do something that was a little scary, would you do it?
- Ask your parents to tell you a story about what they were afraid of when they were little. Ask them if they are afraid of anything now. Do they have a "special star" to help them remember to trust God?